Jan 2020

HARDWOOD GREATS
PRO BASKETBALL'S BEST PLAYERS

RUSSELL WESTBROOK

BY DONALD PARKER

HARDWOOD GREATS

PRO BASKETBALL'S BEST PLAYERS

CHRIS PAUL

GIANNIS ANTETOKOUNMPO

JAMES HARDEN

KEVIN DURANT

LEBRON JAMES

PAUL GEORGE

RUSSELL WESTBROOK

STEPHEN CURRY

HARDWOOD GREATS
PRO BASKETBALL'S BEST PLAYERS

RUSSELL WESTBROOK

DONALD PARKER

MASON CREST
PHILADELPHIA
MIAMI

Mason Crest
450 Parkway Drive, Suite D
Broomall, Pennsylvania 19008
(866) MCP-BOOK (toll-free)
www.masoncrest.com

First printing
9 8 7 6 5 4 3 2 1

ISBN (hardback) 978-1-4222-4351-0
ISBN (series) 978-1-4222- 4344-2
ISBN (ebook) 978-1-4222- 7466-8

Cataloging-in-Publication Data on file with the Library of Congress

Developed and Produced by National Highlights Inc.
Editor: Andrew Luke
Interior and cover design: Annalisa Gumbrecht, Studio Gumbrecht
Production: Michelle Luke

QR CODES AND LINKS TO THIRD-PARTY CONTENT

CONTENTS

KEY ICONS TO LOOK FOR:

Words to Understand: These words with their easy-to-understand definitions will increase the reader's understanding of the text while building vocabulary skills.

Sidebars: This boxed material within the main text allows readers to build knowledge, gain insights, explore possibilities, and broaden their perspectives by weaving together additional information to provide realistic and holistic perspectives.

Educational Videos: Readers can view videos by scanning our QR codes, providing them with additional educational content to supplement the text. Examples include news coverage, moments in history, speeches, iconic sports moments, and much more!

Text-Dependent Questions: These questions send the reader back to the text for more careful attention to the evidence presented there.

Research Projects: Readers are pointed toward areas of further inquiry connected to each chapter. Suggestions are provided for projects that encourage deeper research and analysis.

Series Glossary of Key Terms: This back-of-the-book glossary contains terminology used throughout this series. Words found here increase the reader's ability to read and comprehend higher-level books and articles in this field.

WORDS TO UNDERSTAND

evidenced: Made clear; supported; demonstrated

hallmark: A distinguishing characteristic, trait, or feature

mastery: Possession or display of great skill or technique

workhorse: Something that is markedly useful, durable, or dependable

CHAPTER 1

GREATEST MOMENTS

RUSSELL WESTBROOK'S NBA CAREER

Russell Westbrook knows how to play basketball. He also knows how to dress, claiming to own more than 1,000 pairs of shoes. Whether styling on the court with his play or off with his flashy footwear, Westbrook has established himself as a **workhorse** and one of the game's current superstars. He is as comfortable taking charge of a game and helping his teammates reach their potential as he is modeling one of the many pairs of shoes in his incredible collection.

It is no accident that Westbrook's name contains two Rs, two Ss, two Es, two Ls, and two Os. He is the reigning NBA (National Basketball Association) triple-double leader. A triple-double is achieving double digits in three of the following categories in a game: points, assists, rebounds, steals, or blocks.

The great Oscar Robertson held the previous record for triple-doubles in a season with 41, set in the 1961–62 season with Cincinnati.

During the 2016–2017 NBA season, Westbrook surpassed the 45-year-old record for most triple-doubles in a season set by the great Hall of Fame player Oscar Robertson. He came back in the following season (2017–2018) to become the first player to average a triple-double a game in consecutive seasons.

When he entered the league in 2008 as the fourth overall pick of the Seattle Supersonics (who six days after he was drafted moved to Oklahoma City to become the Thunder), Westbrook played in a trio that featured himself, Kevin Durant, and James Harden, all future NBA Most Valuable Players (MVPs). Westbrook won the league's MVP award in 2017. He was also a member of the U.S. Men's National basketball team that won the gold medal at the 2012 Summer Olympics Game in London.

Westbrook has more than established himself as a player to watch, and as his star continues to rise, more recognition will be given to his talent and ability. He takes on the role of playmaker and brings an all-around game that has not been seen since the days of Robertson. In fact, Westbrook and Robertson are the only players in NBA history to average a triple-double in points, assists, and rebounds for an entire season. Westbrook has taken this accomplishment a step further by repeating it, being the only player to average a triple-double in consecutive seasons.

There is no doubt that at the end of his career, Westbrook will be considered one of the hardest working and best all-around players the NBA has seen. He certainly holds the distinction of being a consistent triple threat when on the court and will continue to be recognized for his talent as he works toward his goal of becoming an NBA champion. This book takes a look at what Westbrook has been able to accomplish in his career so far and how his career compares with that of some of the greatest players to have played in the NBA.

WESTBROOK'S GREATEST CAREER MOMENTS

HERE IS A LIST OF SOME OF THE CAREER

FIRSTS AND GREATEST ACHIEVEMENTS

DURING HIS TIME IN THE NBA:

Westbrook is a triple-double machine, scoring when he can, but also grabbing rebounds and involving teammates often as well.

SCORES 10,000 POINTS FOR A CAREER

Westbrook has averaged 23.0 points a game (through the 2018–2019 NBA season) and is prolific at grabbing rebounds or dishing out assists to his teammates. Near the end of the 2014–2015 season he joined the ranks of players scoring at least 10,000 points in a career during a February 27, 2015 game against the Portland Trailblazers. Westbrook scored 40 points to go along with 13 rebounds and 11 assists for a triple-double. He currently ranks in the top 60 (through the 2018–2019 season) of all players in NBA history in total points scored.

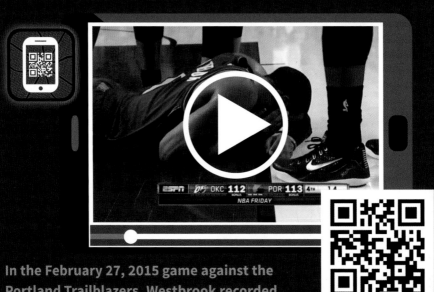

In the February 27, 2015 game against the Portland Trailblazers, Westbrook recorded a triple-double (points-assists-rebounds) on his way to scoring his 10,000th career point in the NBA. This video shows Westbrook hitting his 40th point in the game and suffering a minor facial injury.

MOST TRIPLE-DOUBLES IN A SEASON

The **hallmark** of Westbrook's game is his ability to record a triple-double. This is **evidenced** by the 42 triple-doubles he had in the 2016–2017 NBA season. Westbrook's 42nd triple-double passed the record held for 55 years by Hall-of-Famer and former Cincinnati Royals and Milwaukee Bucks great, Oscar Robertson (who recorded 41, set in the 1961–1962 NBA season).

Westbrook scores 50 points in a game against the Denver Nuggets on April 9, 2017, along with 14 rebounds, and 10 assists. This achievement gave him his 42nd triple-double for the season and the NBA career record. He passed the record set by Hall-of-Famer Oscar Robertson, which stood since the 1961–1962 season.

CONSECUTIVE SEASON TRIPLE-DOUBLE AVERAGE

In addition to setting the career single-season record for triple-doubles (with 42, set in 2017), Westbrook came back in the 2017–2018 NBA season and accomplished something no other player had done before. He averaged a triple-double for two consecutive seasons. Westbrook's ability to score, grab rebounds, and provide assists to his teammates has made him one of the best all-around team players in the league and exciting to watch.

Russell Westbrook: needs 16 rebounds to average a triple-double for the season

Westbrook is featured in a game versus the Memphis Grizzlies on April 11, 2018, where he grabbed 20 rebounds. Although he finished the game with a double-double (six points and 19 assists), the 20 boards were enough for Westbrook to reach an average of a triple-double a game for the 2017–2018 NBA season and to become the first player in league history to do so in consecutive years.

FIRST TIME 50 POINTS SCORED IN A TRIPLE-DOUBLE SINCE 1975

One truly rare accomplishment in Westbrook's career happened on October 28, 2016, in a game against the Phoenix Suns. For the game he scored 51 points, grabbed 13 rebounds, and dished out 10 assists in one of the 42 triple-doubles Westbrook recorded in the record-setting season of 2016–2017. His 51 points was the first time 50 or more points have been scored in a triple-double since Hall of Fame center Kareem Abdul-Jabbar did so in the January 19, 1975 game as a member of the Milwaukee Bucks (in a game versus the Portland Trailblazers, where he also had 11 assists and 15 total rebounds).

Highlights of Westbrook's 51-point triple-double effort against the Phoenix Suns on October 28, 2016.

MOST POINTS SCORED IN A TRIPLE-DOUBLE

    Being the first NBA player since 1975 to score 50 points or more in a triple-double is one impressive accomplishment. Westbrook went beyond that five months later in a March matchup against the Orlando Magic. For the game he scored 57 points, dished out 11 assists, and pulled down 13 rebounds in a 116–106 victory. The 57 points were the most ever for a triple-double. He is also one of two players to have recorded a 50-point triple-double twice in the same season (James Harden is the other player, having done it four times since 2017, including a 60-point triple-double).

This video is a highlight of Westbrook's 57-point triple-double effort against the Orlando Magic in a game on March 29, 2017.

FIRST 50-POINT TRIPLE-DOUBLE IN A PLAYOFF GAME

By now it is clear that Westbrook not only loves to score points, he also likes to pull down rebounds and dish assists to get other teammates involved in the game. His amazing ability to record triple-doubles with such regularity reached a new height in a playoff game against the Houston Rockets. The game, which featured a reunion with Westbrook's former Thunder teammate James Harden, saw him score 51 points to go along with 13 assists and 10 rebounds (Harden also scored 35 points in the game, which the Rockets won 115–111).

Highlights of Westbrook's 51-point, 13-assist, and 10-rebound playoff game against his former teammate James Harden and the Houston Rockets on April 19, 2017. The effort was the highest triple-double points scored in a playoff since Charles Barkley (1993) posted a 43-point triple-double game.

NBA MOST VALUABLE PLAYER AWARD, 2016-2017 SEASON

The 2016–2017 NBA season was one where Westbrook came into his own not only as a great player but also as a superstar in the league. He notched his first season of averaging a triple-double a game (in 81 games played) and received 87.9 percent of the total available votes (1,010) to win his first MVP award. He finished one place ahead of former teammate Harden, who would be the 2017–2018 NBA MVP, and eight places in front of another former teammate, Kevin Durant (who received the MVP award for the 2013–2014 season).

Check out this highlight reel of Westbrook's 2016–2017 season where he averaged 31.6 points per game, 10.4 assists, and 10.7 rebounds on his way to winning the league's MVP award.

THE PERFECT TRIPLE-DOUBLE

It cannot be emphasized enough: When it comes to Russell Westbrook, the man can record triple-doubles. He is the single-season record holder at 42, and one of only two players to average a triple-double in a season. He is the only player to average a triple-double in consecutive seasons. What else can he do to demonstrate his **mastery** of the triple-double? How about the perfect triple-double! In a game against the Philadelphia 76ers he was six for six in field goals and six for six in free throws to score 18 points, 14 assists, and 11 rebounds to become the only player to ever record a perfect triple-double.

This video shows Westbrook's efforts in a March 22, 2017 game versus the Philadelphia 76ers where his 18 points, 11 rebounds, and 14 assists gave him a perfect triple-double, his 35th for the 2016–2017 season.

Westbrook dribbles the ball up the court in a 2015 game against Cleveland.

TEXT-DEPENDENT QUESTIONS

1. Which former NBA player did Westbrook surpass for the most triple-doubles in an NBA season (in 2016–2017)? How many triple-doubles did he record? How many years did the former season record last?

2. Which former NBA player's record for highest points scored in a triple-double did Westbrook surpass during an October 28, 2016 game against the Phoenix Suns? When was the previous record set?

3. What year did Westbrook win the league's Most Valuable Player award? Which former teammate finished second in the MVP voting in the year Westbrook won?

 # RESEARCH PROJECT

Westbrook is well-known throughout the league for his ability to record triple-doubles in points, assists, and rebounds. This ability has led to him setting the season record of 42 triple-doubles in 2017, a record that previously was held for 55 years. Find out who the five other players are in NBA history with at least 10 triple-doubles recorded in a season. Note the year the player achieved their triple-double and the number of years between them and Westbrook's 42 triple-double season.

WORDS TO UNDERSTAND

enshrine: To remember and protect (someone or something that is valuable, admired, etc.)

homage: Something that shows respect or attests to the worth or influence of another

proximity: The quality or state of being close

spurt: To show marked, usually increased, growth, activity, or energy in a short period

uncanny: Being beyond what is normal or expected

CHAPTER 2

THE ROAD TO THE TOP

WESTBROOK'S PLAYER PERFORMANCE

Russell Westbrook III was born in Long Beach, California, on November 12, 1988, to father Russell Westbrook Jr. and mother Shannon Horton. Despite his parents not living together, Westbrook learned a strong sense of family from them. He stays in touch with both his mother and father during the season, maintaining his connection to his roots. He also has a younger brother named Raynard, and with his wife, Nina, is the parent of a son named Noah.

Westbrook began developing a love for the game of basketball while he was young, although it took a while for him to eventually grow into his current size of six feet three inches (1.90 m) and 200 pounds (90 kg). Not highly regarded as a recruit coming out of high school, Westbrook eventually received the attention of the University of California at Los Angeles (UCLA, nickname "Bruins") where he excelled and was able to become one of the top picks in the 2008 NBA draft.

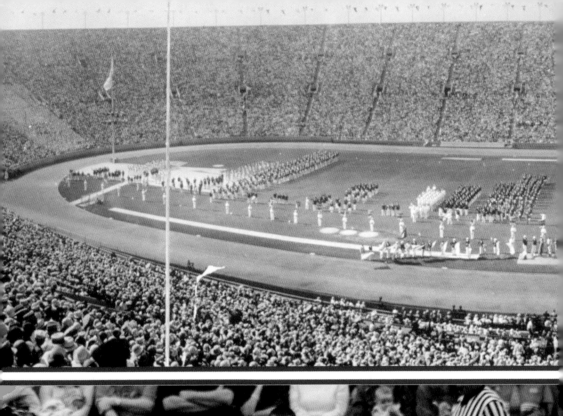

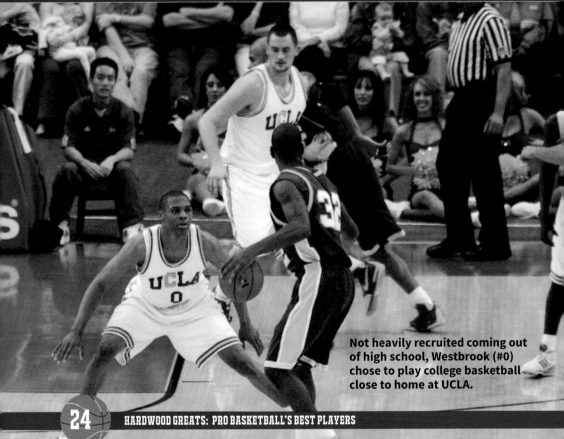

Not heavily recruited coming out of high school, Westbrook (#0) chose to play college basketball close to home at UCLA.

Westbrook's high school team at Leuzinger High School in Lawndale, CA, was nicknamed the Olympians due to its proximity to the Los Angeles Memorial Coliseum, seen here on opening day of the 1932 Summer Olympic Games.

Since entering the league as a member of the Seattle Supersonics (who, afterward, almost immediately became the Oklahoma City Thunder), Westbrook has zoomed to the top of the league and has established himself as a star and potential future Hall of Fame member. In addition to earning MVP honors for the 2016–2017 season, Westbrook has been a member of seven All-Star teams and was named MVP of the All-Star game twice. He has been named to the All-NBA Team (first or second team) in each season from 2011–2018, except for the 2013–2014 season, which was shortened by injury.

Westbrook was also a member of the 2008–2009 All-Rookie Team and was twice named Rookie of the Month for the Western Conference in December 2008 and February 2009. His **uncanny** ability to score, pass, and take the ball off the boards makes him one of the most complete offensive players in NBA history. There is little doubt that by the time he decides to hang up his shoes (one of the 1,000 pairs that he owns), he will be **enshrined** among the game's greats as a member of the NBA Hall of Fame in Springfield, Massachusetts.

NBA DRAFT DAY 2008 SIGNIFICANT ACCOUNTS

- Russell Westbrook was selected by the Seattle Supersonics with the fourth overall pick in the first round of the 2008 NBA draft. The Memphis Grizzlies selected Westbrook's college teammate (at the University of California at Los Angeles) Kevin Love with the fifth overall pick.

- The 2008 NBA draft was held

at Madison Square Garden, located in New York City, on June 26, 2008.

- The Seattle Supersonics selected six players in the 2008 draft, which was their last as the Sonics; the team moved to Oklahoma City to become the Thunder for the 2008–2009 NBA season six days after the draft.

- Westbrook was one of 15 guards taken in the 2008 NBA draft (out of the 60 players drafted in rounds 1 and 2).

- The guard position was the smallest group drafted in the 2008 draft. A total of 21 forwards and 24 centers was also drafted in 2008.

- Derrick Rose, a guard from the University of Memphis, was the first overall selection, drafted by the Chicago Bulls. He went on to be named Rookie of the Year.

- For the first time in NBA draft history, freshmen were drafted with the top three picks (Kansas State's Michael Beasley went to Miami, and University of Southern California's O.J. Mayo went to Minnesota).

- Ten freshmen were taken in the first round, with a record 12 drafted altogether.

Source: https://stats.nba.com/draft/history/?Season=2008—
NBA draft information for 2008 NBA Draft.

ATHLETIC ACCOMPLISHMENTS IN HIGH SCHOOL AND COLLEGE

Early in life, Westbrook had a desire to play in the NBA. His dream of being a professional basketball player was challenged, in part, by Westbrook's undersized frame of five feet eight inches (1.73 m) and a weight of only 140 pounds (64 kg). There was no guessing by his slight build that he would grow to a competitive weight and height and be able to excel on the professional level for more than a decade.

Westbrook had to work harder than most players who had a real chance of becoming a professional-level basketball player. Although he was born in the city of Long Beach, California, Westbrook was raised on the tough streets of South Central Los Angeles. Basketball became an escape for him as he worked to develop the skills he would need to become not only a premier scorer in the NBA but also a leader in assists and rebounds.

Westbrook used an opportunity to attend Leuzinger High School (nickname, "Olympians") in Lawndale, California, located in the Los Angeles inner-city community called Inglewood. The school received its nickname "Olympians" because of its **proximity** to the site of the 1932 Summer Olympic Games in Los Angeles.

High School

Westbrook entered Leuzinger High School ("Olympians") in 2002. A bit undersized as compared to teammates his age, he did not play in his first two years while attending the school. He became a member of the varsity team in

The crowd at Pauley Pavilion, where Westbrook played his college basketball for UCLA, cheers on its team.

2004 during his junior year, and by his senior year in 2005, he was averaging 25.1 points per game. Between his freshman and senior years, he experienced enough of a growth **spurt** to receive some interest from colleges around the country.

Here are Westbrook's numbers for the years he played basketball at Leuzinger High School:

Year (G)	PTS	PPG	FGM	2PTM	3PTM	FTM/A	FT%	TREB
2002–2003 (0)				Did not play				
2003–2004 (0)				Did not play				
2004–2005 (24)	288	12.0	109	98	11	54/77	70.1	113
2005–2006 (28)	704	25.1	237	180	57	173/228	75.9	244
TOTALS (52)	**992**	**19.1**	**346**	**278**	**68**	**227/305**	**74.4**	**357**

Westbrook did not receive many offers to attend college on a basketball scholarship, but he caught the attention of UCLA Bruins men's basketball then-head coach Ben Howland. Howland was impressed enough with his offensive skill and ability to play as an all-around player that he offered him a chance to become a member of the Bruins basketball team, which Westbrook accepted.

THE MEANING BEHIND THE INITIALS ON HIS SHOES

If you look closely at Westbrook's shoes during an NBA game, you will notice the initials "KB3" written in marker near the sole in the middle of the outer side of each sneaker. The initials hold a special meaning for him as they are meant to honor the memory of his childhood friend, Khelcey Barrs III. They played basketball together in high school with dreams of playing at UCLA. Barrs died of cardiac arrest during a regular pickup game in his sophomore year.

This video has Westbrook discussing the importance of the initials "KB3" on his sneakers as an homage to his childhood friend Khelcey Barrs III, who passed away at the young age of sixteen.

College

Westbrook entered college at the University of California at Los Angeles (UCLA) in the fall of 2006. His start at UCLA was less than memorable. In the 36 games he played for the Bruins in the 2006–2007 season, he scored 122 points for an average per game (ppg) of 3.4. Westbrook stepped up his game in his sophomore year, scoring nearly 500 points in 39 games for a 12.7 ppg.

Here are the numbers for his two seasons at UCLA (including NCAA tournament games):

Year (G)	PTS	PPG	FGM	2PTM	3PTM	FTM/A	FT%	TREB
2006–2007 (36)	122	3.4	48	39	9	17/31	.548	28
2007–2008 (39)	497	12.7	182	156	26	107/150	.713	153
TOTALS (75)	**619**	**8.3**	**230**	**195**	**35**	**124/181**	**.685**	**181**

At the end of his sophomore year, Westbrook entered the 2008 NBA draft along with fellow UCLA teammate Kevin Love (who was selected by the Memphis Grizzlies with the pick after his selection, number five overall in the first round). Westbrook's selection with the fourth pick by the Seattle Supersonics made him one of the last players Seattle would select before their move to become the Oklahoma City Thunder a week after the draft.

Westbrook's UCLA teammate Kevin Love also entered the 2008 NBA draft and was selected immediately after Westbrook.

RUSSELL WESTBROOK AND OKLAHOMA CITY'S BIG THREE

While playing in Oklahoma City, Westbrook joined Kevin Durant, who was drafted by the Seattle Supersonics in 2007. The pair played together for nine seasons, from 2008 (when Westbrook was drafted) through the end of 2016, when Durant left for Golden State. James Harden was drafted from Arizona State University by the Thunder in 2009 and played with Westbrook and Durant for three seasons before being traded to the Houston Rockets.

During their time together, the trio of future MVPs played in a total of 676 games, scored 13,951 points (for a per-game average of 20.6 for the three), had 3,515 rebounds (4.3 per game), and 2902 assists (5.2 per game).

Season	Player	GP	PTS	PPG	REB	ASST
2009–2010	Westbrook	82	1,322	16.1	401	652
	Durant	82	2,472	30.1	623	231
	Harden	76	753	9.9	244	137
2010–2011	Westbrook	82	1,793	21.9	379	670
	Durant	78	2,161	27.7	533	214
	Harden	82	998	12.2	255	176
2011–2012*	Westbrook	66	1,558	23.6	301	362
	Durant	66	1,850	28.0	527	231
	Harden	62	1,044	16.8	252	229
	TOTALS	676	13,951	20.6	3,515	2,902

*The 2011–2012 NBA season was shortened due to a league lockout, reducing the regular season to 50 games.

Westbrook and Durant played together for 8 seasons before Durant left for Golden State.

The OKC Big Three played in the 2012 NBA Championship series against the Eastern Conference champion Miami Heat's Big Three of LeBron James, Dwyane Wade, and Chris Bosh. The Heat won the series four games to one in what is to date Westbrook's only appearance in an NBA Final. The Thunder trio played in all five games for a total of 117.7 minutes played. Durant, Harden, and Westbrook, respectively, averaged 30.6, 12.4, and 27.0 points per game in the 2012 Finals.

Westbrook and the Thunder lost to Miami's Big Three of Dwyane Wade (L), LeBron James, and Chris Bosh (R) in the 2012 NBA Finals.

Here are the numbers for the 2012 NBA Finals where the Thunder Three met the Heat Three for the championship:

Player	GP	PTS	PPG	REB	ASST
Westbrook	**5**	**135**	**27.0**	**32**	**33**
Durant	5	153	30.6	30	11
Harden	5	62	12.4	24	18
TOTALS	**15**	**350**	**23.3**	**86**	**62**
James	5	143	28.6	51	37
Wade	5	113	22.6	30	26
Bosh	5	73	14.6	47	1
TOTALS	**15**	**329**	**21.9**	**128**	**64**

The numbers show the two trios were very competitive, but the Heat stars had a significant edge in rebounding. Clearly Westbrook and his teammates did not lose due to a lack of production from him and their best players.

Here's how the three OKC players compare to each other over their careers:

Player	PTS	PPG	FGM	FG%	3PTM	3PT%	FTM	FT%
Kevin Durant	22,940	27.0	7,814	49.3%	1570	38.1%	5742	88.3%
Russell Westbrook	**18,859**	**23.0**	**6,626**	**43.4%**	**922**	**30.8%**	**4685**	**80.1%**
James Harden	18,627	24.3	5,499	44.3%	2,025	36.5%	5,604	85.7%

There is no telling how many more opportunities Oklahoma City's Big Three would have had if they stayed together after the 2012 season, when Harden left. Would they have had a chance to face Miami's Big Three one more time in the NBA Finals? Separately, Westbrook, Durant, and Harden have risen to NBA superstardom. It is clear that their time together formed the foundation of this rise. In 2019, Oklahoma City traded Westbrook to Houston, where he was reunited with fellow MVP Harden.

Kevin Durant has gone on to incredible success since he left OKC and Westbrook.

Westbrook started wearing 0 when he went to UCLA because to him it represented a new beginning.

TEXT-DEPENDENT QUESTIONS

1. What are the names of the other members of Oklahoma City's Big Three that played together through the 2011–2012 season? What was the name of the team whose Big Three they faced in the 2012 NBA Finals?

2. What initials are written on Westbrook's shoes? What is the significance of these initials?

3. In what college class year (i.e., freshman, sophomore, junior, or senior) did Westbrook decide to enter the NBA draft? How many years did he play college basketball for UCLA?

 RESEARCH PROJECT

Russell Westbrook and his UCLA teammate Kevin Love were selected with the fourth and fifth pick of the 2008 NBA draft. It is rare for college teammates to be drafted in consecutive order, but it has happened. Going as far back as the 1990 draft, find at least three additional pairs of college teammates who were drafted in consecutive order (in either rounds 1 or 2).

WORDS TO UNDERSTAND

by virtue of: Through the force of; by authority of

durable: Able to exist for a long time without significant deterioration in quality or value

undisputed: Without question or argument

ON THE COURT

RUSSELL WESTBROOK'S NBA ACCOMPLISHMENTS

Russell Westbrook has more than established himself as a premier player in the NBA. He played alongside two other potential future Hall-of-Fame players, James Harden (Houston Rockets) and Kevin Durant (Golden State Warriors), in the beginning of his career. After their respective departures, Westbrook (who joined Harden in the Houston backcourt for the 2019–2020 season) stepped up in his role as team leader. Westbrook guided the Thunder, post–Durant and –Harden (2016–2019), as the team's **undisputed** go-to player. He posted the following numbers in that role, leading the team to a 144-102 win/loss record (as compared to the numbers put up by his two former teammates):

James Harden left Oklahoma City to join Houston following the 2011–2012 season.

Russell Westbrook *(Oklahoma City Thunder, one MVP Award)*

Season	GP	PTS	PPG	REB	ASST	PLAYOFF WINS
2016–2017	81	2,558	31.6	864	840	1
2017–2018	80	2,028	25.4	804	820	2
2018-2019	73	1,675	22.9	807	784	1
TOTALS	**234**	**6,261**	**26.8**	**2,475**	**2,444**	**4**

James Harden *(Houston Rockets, one MVP Award)*

Season	GP	PTS	PPG	REB	ASST	PLAYOFF WINS
2016–2017	81	2,356	29.1	659	907	6
2017–2018	72	2,191	30.4	389	630	11
2018-2019	78	2,818	36.1	518	586	6
TOTALS	**231**	**7,022**	**24.3**	**1,566**	**2,123**	**23**

RUSSELL WESTBROOK

POINT GUARD

- Date of birth: November 12, 1988

- Height: six feet three inches (1.90 m); weight: 200 pounds (90 kg)

- Drafted in the first round of the 2008 NBA draft (fourth pick overall) by the Seattle Supersonics (now Oklahoma City Thunder)

- College: University of California at Los Angeles (Nickname: "Bruins")

- Named the 2017 NBA Most Valuable Player

- Two-time NBA scoring champion (2015, 2017)

- Two-time NBA assists leader (2018, 2019)

- Eight-time NBA All-Star (2011–2013, 2015–2019)

- Two-time All-NBA first team

- Pac-10 Defensive Player of the Year at UCLA (2008)

Kevin Durant *(Golden State Warriors, 1 MVP Award, 2 NBA Championships)*

Season	GP	PTS	PPG	REB	ASST	PLAYOFF WINS
2016–2017	62	1,555	25.1	513	300	14*†
2017–2018	68	1,792	26.4	464	366	16‡
2018-2019	78	2,027	26.0	497	457	8*
TOTALS	**208**	**5,374**	**25.8**	**1,474**	**1,123**	**44**

*Durant was injured for two of 16 wins in 2017 and for six of 14 wins in 2019.
†Golden State won the 2017 NBA Championship, 4–1, over the Cleveland Cavaliers.
‡Golden State won the 2018 NBA Championship, 4–0, over the Cleveland Cavaliers.

 # BECOMING THE LEAGUE'S MVP

Westbrook had quite a 2016–2017 season. He broke Oscar Robertson's single-season record for triple-doubles, which had been held since the 1961–1962 season. Westbrook also secured the first "perfect" triple-double in NBA history by going a perfect six for six from the field and making all six of his free throws in a March 22, 2017 game against the Philadelphia 76ers. He also finished the season averaging a triple-double, something that only Robertson had done. These accomplishments helped pave the way to him winning his first league MVP award.

Westbrook was named the NBA Most Valuable Player for the 2016–2017 season.

HALLMARKS OF WESTBROOK'S CAREER

Although Westbrook was selected with the fourth pick in the 2008 draft, the expectation for his play was never as high as it was for his teammate, second overall pick Kevin Durant. This was particularly hard for Westbrook during the years he and Durant played together, as Westbrook's ability to make plays and lead often conflicted with the slow and steady style of Durant, to whom the team often deferred. Westbrook has blossomed since the departure of Durant.

One of the things that Westbrook has been able to accomplish in his career includes being named to eight NBA All-Star Games, from 2011–2013 and 2015–2019. He is also a two-time NBA All-League first team member (2016, 2017) and five-time second team selection (2011–2013, 2015, 2018). Since 2014 he has finished in the top five for MVP voting each season, winning the award in 2017.

Highlights of the various plays throughout the 2016–2017 NBA season that gave Westbrook his first career league MVP award.

Westbrook is an eight-time NBA All-Star and two-time All-NBA first team selection.

Westbrook has been remarkably durable in his career, missing four or fewer games in eight of his first 11 seasons.

Westbrook is certainly a **durable** player, having been in the top two for games played beginning with his rookie year (2008–2009) through the 2012–2013 season. As a rookie, Westbrook was named to the NBA All-Rookie team and became the league's MVP in 2017. He has also taken home a number of weekly and monthly awards, and there is no telling how many more awards Westbrook will acquire before his NBA career comes to an end.

HOW WESTBROOK RANKS

Westbrook ranks high on different lists for all-time and current NBA players in several categories, including:

Most Triple-Doubles *(Career)*

Player Name	Number of Seasons
Oscar Robertson*	181
Magic Johnson*	138
Russell Westbrook†	*138*
Jason Kidd*	107
LeBron James†	81
Wilt Chamberlain	78
Larry Bird*	59
Fat Lever	43
James Harden†	42
Bob Cousy*	33

*Member of the NBA Hall of Fame
†Active player (as of 2018–2019 season)

Most 50-Point Games *(Career-Active Players)*

Player Name	Number of Games
James Harden	18
LeBron James	12
Stephen Curry	6
Kevin Durant	6
Russell Westbrook	*5*

Westbrook has a long way to go to catch the legendary Oscar Robertson in career triple-doubles.

2010 FIBA CHAMPIONSHIPS

Westbrook was named to the U.S. Men's National team in 2010 and participated in the International Basketball Federation's (FIBA) World Cup Championship. Turkey, the host country, held the championship from August 28 to September 12, 2010, in the historic city of Istanbul. Players for the 24 qualifying teams came from various national professional and semiprofessional leagues (including the NBA and NCAA). Forty-nine players representing the NBA played on the various international squads, making it the most represented international league at the tournament.

Joining Westbrook on the squad was then-teammate Kevin Durant, and 2008 NBA Rookie of the Year Derrick Rose. His UCLA teammate Kevin Love, then a member of the Minnesota Timberwolves, was also a member of the team in the center position.

For his part, representing the United States in his first international competition, Westbrook scored 82 points in the nine games he played for a per-game average of 9.1. His contributions (along with teammate Durant who led all American players with 205 total points, scoring 22.8 points per game) helped lead the U.S. to a 81–64 victory over host Turkey to win the championship. In that game, coming off the bench, Westbrook scored 13 points (third among U.S. players, behind Lamar Odom who scored 15 and Durant who led all with 28 points) to go with six rebounds and three assists in 26 minutes of play.

THE 2012 LONDON SUMMER OLYMPICS

Following up on his play in Istanbul at the World Championships in 2010, Westbrook was named to continue to represent the U.S. at the 2012 Summer Olympics game in London. The United States, **by virtue of** its win in 2010 at the FIBA championship, became one of 12 teams to be invited to play in the Summer Olympics. The other qualifying teams were Tunisia (winner of the FIBA African Championship), Argentina and Brazil (representing the FIBA Americas Championship), Australia (2011 FIBA Oceania Championship), Spain and France (from the FIBA Europe Championship), and China (2011 FIBA Asia Championship). Lithuania, Russia, and Nigeria won qualifying games to make up teams nine to 11, and Great Britain, as the host nation, received a qualifying spot.

Durant and Love, Westbrook's former NBA and UCLA teammates, again joined him on the team, as did James Harden (who at the time had just left the Thunder to join the Houston Rockets). Other players rounding out the

Westbrook played for Team USA at the 2012 Summer Olympic Games.

U.S. squad included Kobe Bryant, Chris Paul, Carmelo Anthony, and LeBron James. The U.S. team swept through the other teams, posting a perfect 8–0 record and winning the gold medal. How well did Westbrook play? He scored a total of 68 points for an average per game of 8.5, with 13 assists, 13 rebounds, and seven steals.

TEXT-DEPENDENT QUESTIONS

1. Where does Westbrook rank on the career list for triple-doubles? Where does he rank on the single-season list for triple-doubles?

2. How many NBA scoring titles does Westbrook have?

3. How many NBA players participated in the 2010 FIBA World Cup held in Turkey?

RESEARCH PROJECT

Playing on a team with two other superstars can be difficult for other players, but for Westbrook it helped him further shape his pro game and become even better. His being named the league's MVP for the 2016–2017 season evidenced this. This honor was followed up by former teammate James Harden being recognized as MVP in 2017–2018. With Kevin Durant having won MVP in 2014, they are the only former teammates to have achieved this honor within a five-year period. There is only one other instance where players who were once on the same team won the league's MVP award while playing for another team. Find out who those two players are, the year(s) that they won the award, and the team they represented.

WORDS TO UNDERSTAND

budding: At an early stage of development, but showing promise or potential

obsession: The domination of one's thoughts or feelings by a persistent idea, image, desire, etc.

opt: To make a choice

CHAPTER 4

WORDS COUNT

When the time comes to address the media before or after a game, players either retreat to the comfort of traditional phrases that avoid controversy (Cliché City), or they speak their mind with refreshing candor (Quote Machine).

Here are 10 quotes, compiled in part from the website AZquotes.com, with some insight as to the context of what Westbrook is talking about or referencing:

"**There's no reason to hold yourself back and say you can't do something in life unless you go for it and try to do it.**"

Westbrook overcame a slow start at the beginning of his collegiate career, growing into a player to watch in the NBA. He needed the growth spurt he experienced during his senior year in high school, which saw him grow from five feet eight inches (1.73 m) to near his present height of six feet three inches (1.90 m) to trigger his development. Westbrook's eventual selection as the fourth pick in the 2008 NBA draft is often attributed to his determination in the face of adversity. He has overcome challenges that he has faced in his life by challenging those who told him he could not do something. Unfortunately, at the time of this quote no one challenged Westbrook to express this in a more original way. **Rating: Cliché City**

Westbrook overcame naysayers and doubters to turn one good year in college into an outstanding NBA career.

"I've always had to prove myself to people growing up. I had to show them that I could do this and I could do that and paying no mind to what the critics said."

Westbrook did not grow up as the biggest, fastest, or strongest player on the court. The skills he has developed on the court came through practice, hard work, dedication, and a desire to prove that others were wrong about him. He was not highly recruited coming out high school even though he led his team to a 25–4 record in his senior year—but he did enough to catch the attention of UCLA and earn himself a chance to play college basketball. He did not have a great freshman year at UCLA but excelled in the following year to catch the attention of NBA scouts and get drafted in the first round. He played on a team with two other superstars (Durant and Harden) but carved out his own way and earned MVP honors. Despite what critics may say about him, he has overcome their criticism and shown that he has the ability to become great. The only criticism now might be for lack of originality in quotes. **Rating: Cliché City**

> **"I'm never satisfied. I'm always trying to get better and learn from my mistakes."**

It would be very easy for Westbrook to be satisfied with all that he has so far accomplished in his NBA career, including several Western Conference Finals appearances, one NBA Final appearance, and winning the league's MVP award. His projected career numbers rank him among the best players to have played in the league. His ability to record triple-doubles and average one for an entire season (twice) ranks him alongside Hall-of-Fame inductee Oscar Robertson as the only players with that accomplishment. All of this is of little importance to Westbrook, however, as his goal is to always accomplish more than he has in the past. Westbrook will not be satisfied until he wins a championship. Hopefully he will continue to strive toward offering less well-worn quotes. **Rating: Cliché City**

Despite all his success on the basketball court, Westbrook continues to work on improving as he chases that elusive NBA championship.

"Be yourself. It's the most important part of anything that you do. It's not fashion. It can be whatever you want to do."

Westbrook promotes the idea that the most important thing that you can be in life is true to yourself. It does not matter if that means becoming an NBA star like Westbrook, a fashion model, a world-class surgeon, or a clerk in a law office. Whatever it is you are looking to accomplish in life, develop your skills, build your knowledge, and pursue it with passion. If you are true to who you are and put in hard work, you should find the success and happiness you desire in life. A very true sentiment, but we have heard it before. **Rating: Cliché City**

> ## "Every day when I get on the floor I give it my all and play because you never know what tomorrow holds."

Westbrook has been in the league since 2008, which is a lot of years playing a physically demanding sport. He feels blessed that he has been given an opportunity that not many people are given in life, and he looks to make the most of his time on the basketball court. He is saying he gives 100 percent effort, a common cliché, because Westbrook fully understands that there is no guarantee that he will have the same opportunity to perform tomorrow. **Rating: Cliché City**

Westbrook defends against Kobe Bryant at a Team USA practice in 2012.

> "Once you put in all the work prepractice and postpractice and see it in a game and see it in play, that's a great feeling."

Hard work through practice pays off. This is also a cliché, but there is a lot of truth in this expression. Westbrook, unlike some professional athletes who do not believe in practicing, knows that his skills are developed when he has the chance to repeat drills, simulate different game situations, and work on his fundamental skills. He puts in the work before and after games so that when he is in a game situation, everything comes together effortlessly. Being able to see the fruits of his labor come together when on the court with his teammates is the biggest payoff for Westbrook. **Rating: Cliché City**

> "The game will tell you what to do on the floor, and that's what I try to do."

Westbrook is the only player in NBA history to record back-to-back seasons averaging a triple-double per game. This means that he is more than a one-dimensional player who only concentrates on scoring baskets. He uses the game as his guide to tell him what role he should take as leader of the Houston Rockets.

If the flow of the game allows for him to take more shots, he will do so without hesitation. If he knows that he is not having a particularly good night from the floor, it's better to pass the ball to other teammates to get them involved. He is not afraid to crash the boards and pull down rebounds in order to keep a scoring opportunity alive or deny the other team a chance to score. His ability to do all three of these things at once clearly shows that he has a keen awareness on the court and the ability to adapt to the right role at the right time. **Rating: Quote Machine**

> **"My childhood, I wouldn't say it was bad. It helped me grow up. I stayed out of trouble. My parents taught me what's wrong and right, and knowing that I had a little brother following me, I had to make sure I was doing the right thing so he knows what's right, too. I was in the house nine days out of 10. There wasn't nothing good outside for me."**

Westbrook was raised mostly by his mother, although both parents were involved in his life. Growing up mostly in the rough South Central section of Los Angeles, he stayed focused on one day attending UCLA to play basketball—which he did—setting a good example for his younger brother, Raynard, and doing what he could to further develop into a great NBA player—which he has. The rough nature of his childhood neighborhood, with its many bad influences, motivated him to stay out of trouble and focus on his and his brother's well-being. He learned early on that leading by example and staying away from the negative influences that surround you is the only way to keep out of trouble and thrive in life.

Rating: Quote Machine

With gangs and other bad influences prevalent in the South Central LA neighborhood he grew up in, Westbrook knew he had to stay focused to stay out of trouble.

At the 2017 ESPY Awards, Westbrook chose black wingtips with red laces adorned with silver ornamentation as his footwear statement.

"I have a certain taste, and I might be like, 'I like this,' when other people are like, 'I can't wear that.' And in basketball, I might be able to do things other guys might not."

There is no doubt that Westbrook has developed all-around skills. He is the reigning triple-double champion, being one of two players to average one over an entire NBA season. His ability to score, assist, and rebound means that he is willing to take on whatever role is needed for his team to win. In this quote he equates his willingness to take fashion risks with his willingness to assume the role needed by his team on a given night—he might score, he might help his teammates score, he might rebound the ball and give his team a chance to score. His willingness to adapt means that he is willing to take roles that other players may not want.

Rating: Quote Machine

"Shoes make an outfit. You can throw on a crazy shirt and crazy pants, but you add those shoes—done."

It is no secret that Russell Westbrook loves shoes. Whether the count of his current collection is 100, the reported 1,000, or 1,000,000, the man simply loves shoes. This quote speaks not only to his love for shoes but also his attention to detail and how a good pair of shoes may be all you need to make an outfit work. His **obsession** with shoes is something that is well known throughout the league and even the source of jokes at his expense. **Rating: Quote Machine**

THE RELATIONSHIP BETWEEN WESTBROOK AND DURANT

It is one thing to play on a team with one **budding** superstar and quite another to have two or three potential Hall-of-Fame players on the same squad. Such was the case for Westbrook, as he was first a member of a trio in Oklahoma City with James Harden and Kevin Durant, and then part of the Westbrook/Durant duo for four additional years after Harden **opted** not to re-sign with OKC at the end of the 2012 season. Toward the end of Durant's time in Oklahoma City, much was made about the problems between the two. The fracture that was being created between the two teammates was enough to help Durant decide to join the Golden State Warriors in 2016. The two have made an attempt to repair their relationship and set aside their old differences for the sake of a renewed friendship.

This short video chronicles the animosity that developed between the two stars after Durant went to Golden State.

RUSSELL WESTBROOK AND THE ORIGIN OF "WHY NOT?"

"Why not?" is a question that Russell Westbrook learned to ask early on in his life (more on this in Chapter 5). Due to his constant questioning, he has faced challenges with a desire to not only overcome them but also show that he could set aside criticism about him and his ability. Westbrook didn't grow up in a life of privilege or with many resources. He did, however, grow up with a tremendous sense of identity and what he could accomplish in life.

Westbrook did not let the negative influences around him discourage or tempt him. He remained focused on his goals in life and moving toward things that were positive and encouraging. That is not to say that he did not engage in silly pranks or do what he refers to in a *USA Today* sports article as "dumb stuff." He further explains in the article:

"It started off back in high school, my friends and I were just doing a lot of dumb stuff—throwing each other's backpacks, or not going to class. So for months, every day we'd say that—'Why not?' It would be some dumb [stuff] like, 'Let's run in the middle of the street'—'Why not?' 'Let's go over here'—'Why not?' 'Let's go out'—'Why not?' We all played basketball together and before the game we'd be like, 'Pssh, why not? Let's hoop. Who cares?'

"Then me and my real close friend thought, this is something that we can use—being kids growing up in the inner city, giving other kids a sense of confidence, a sense of swagger. I didn't think I'd be playing in the NBA at the time, but just being able to give the next person, your brother, your friend, whoever it is, some confidence. Why not? Who told you [that] you can't? That's how it started, and now I'm using the mantra to keep impacting people across the world."

Clearly, these words have been a motivating force in his life and something that has guided him throughout not only his NBA career but also his life.

TEXT-DEPENDENT QUESTIONS

1. How many pairs of shoes does Westbrook own (reportedly)?

2. What part of Los Angeles did Russell Westbrook grow up in?

3. How tall was Westbrook at the beginning of his senior year in high school? How tall was he when began playing basketball at UCLA in 2006?

 # RESEARCH PROJECT

Westbrook is one of a few players in league history to play two (or less) years in college and become the NBA's Most Valuable Player. This is even more remarkable considering the fact that he grew seven inches (0.17 m) and gained 60 pounds (26 kg) in his senior year of high school, finally reaching his present height and weight. Find five other players who either left school early or went straight from high school to later be named MVP.

WORDS TO UNDERSTAND

manifest: To make clear or evident to the eye or the understanding; show plainly

premise: A basis, stated or assumed, on which reasoning proceeds

professes: To declare openly; announce or affirm; avow or acknowledge

CHAPTER 5

OFF THE COURT

AT HOME WITH WESTBROOK

Westbrook's life consists not only of his time on the court with his teammates and coaches but also time off the court (and in the off-season) with his wife Nina Earl, and their toddler son, Noah. The couple, who met as students while attending UCLA (she played basketball for the Lady Bruins), married on August 30, 2015. It was announced in November of 2018 that the Westbrooks welcomed twin girls Jordyn and Skye as the newest additions to their family.

Westbrook was born in Long Beach, California, was raised in South Central LA, and attended school at UCLA, located in the city's Westwood neighborhood. It is only fitting that he decided to establish roots in the city where he was raised and educated. Westbrook purchased a newly built house

Westbrook and his wife, Nina, live in the Los Angeles area town of Brentwood with their three children.

in the city's Brentwood neighborhood for nearly $20 million. The new home makes him neighbors with another one of the Los Angeles area's newest celebrities, LeBron James.

WESTBROOK AND EDUCATION

Westbrook was recruited to attend UCLA to play basketball in 2006 for coach Ben Howland and the Bruins program. He attended the school for two years before declaring himself eligible for the 2008 NBA draft. Westbrook did not finish his studies at UCLA but has shown a commitment toward providing educational opportunities for those in need.

Westbrook sided with teachers in Oklahoma who walked out of the classroom in spring 2018 in a dispute with the government over wages. When asked about supporting the teachers walking out of the classroom, Westbrook was quoted as saying "I'm definitely all in for that." He further explained:

"Education is very important to me, and the teachers are standing up for something I obviously believe in: that's helping the kids get a better education."

Westbrook sees education as a way to "level the playing field" and provide opportunities for those youths living in underserved communities. He places great emphasis on literacy as one way that children can sharpen their skills and reach for their personal goals and dreams (answering the question "Why not?").

WESTBROOK IN THE COMMUNITY

Westbrook started the Russell Westbrook Why Not? Foundation in 2012. The primary mission of the foundation is to work with children in communities of need to provide them with the tools to overcome hardship and excel in life. The basic **premise** behind the foundation is a question his parents used to pose to him and his brother as they were growing up. Whenever faced with a challenge and told that they could not achieve a goal or do something because it may be too challenging, they were taught to ask the question "Why not?"

The foundation is engaged in various community-building activities focused on the lives of children in the Oklahoma City area, throughout the state of Oklahoma, and those in the Los Angeles area where Westbrook grew up. One pet project for which he has directly provided funding is the building of reading rooms at various elementary schools in the two cities. After starting the program in 2015, by the spring of 2017, he had funded the building of nearly 20 such facilities in the Oklahoma City area alone.

Westbrook is an enthusiastic advocate for children's literacy, and his foundation has built and funded several reading rooms in schools across Oklahoma City.

The foundation sponsors holiday gatherings for children and their families around Thanksgiving and Christmas. It sponsors bowling gatherings and other events designed to engage youth and talk to them about excelling in academics, and it also matches parents with additional services and aid necessary for building strong families and strong communities.

RUSSELL'S READING ROOMS

Westbrook has led the charge in promoting literacy among youth in Oklahoma City elementary schools by having his foundation invest in the creation of libraries called "Russell's Reading Room." He **professes** a love for reading and wants to share that love with children. This has **manifested** itself in the creation of 20 reading rooms (so far) in Oklahoma City.

Westbrook discusses the opening of his 10th "Russell's Reading Room" at Adams Elementary School in Oklahoma City, Oklahoma.

MARKETING RUSSELL WESTBROOK

In 2017, Westbrook signed a contract extension to remain a member of the Oklahoma City Thunder. The new contract, worth a reported $205 million, is good through the 2021–2022 season. The Rockets are now responsible for the remaining years of the deal. With his trade to Houston in 2019, Westbrook became the last player from the 2008 NBA draft to leave the team that originally picked him.

Thad Foucher of the Wasserman Media Group (WMG) represents him. Foucher, who is WMG's executive vice president, is considered one of the league's super agents. He represents several players in the NBA, including Kyle Anderson of the Memphis Grizzlies and Melvin Frazier Jr. of the Orlando Magic.

Westbrook signed a new contract with the Thunder in 2017 worth more than $200 million.

Additionally, Foucher was able to help Westbrook negotiate his shoe deal with Nike's Air Jordan brand line. The 10-year deal includes his lifestyle signature shoes and the Why Not Zer0.1 brand. The Why Not Zer0.1 is the first-of-its-kind performance shoe that has been connected with the Air Jordan brand. His annual salary of $28.6 million in combination with annual endorsements of $19 million ranked him 51st on the Forbes's Celebrity 100 earnings list in 2018.

Some of the key endorsement deals that he has acquired through the years include:

- Nike
- PepsiCo
- Samsung Electronics
- True Religion Apparel

Westbrook is passionate about fashion, and has worked on designs with Barney's of New York to create his XO collection.

WESTBROOK THE FASHION DESIGNER

One of Westbrook's quotes explains much about his thoughts on how a good pair of shoes can make any outfit, even a bad one, look good. He backs this up through his interest in fashion and a fashion line he created called Made-In-LA clothing. His interest in designing and creating fashion saw him modeling many of the items in his line at the famous Paris Fashion Week.

He has worked with Nike as well as fashion house Barney's of New York and even published a book through publisher Rizzoli titled, *Russell Westbrook:*

Style Drivers. It is not unusual to see his face and styles gracing the pages of magazines such as *Vogue*, *GQ*, and the style section of the *New York Times*. The interest in fashion has also given birth to a fashion brand that was launched in November 2017. The brand, known as Honor The Gift, plays on his Why Not? theme and pays tribute to the belief he has in himself and a dedication to continue to develop and honor the gifts that he has been blessed.

His Inner City line pays respect to the tough Hawthorne section of South Central Los Angeles where he grew up and is designed to provide simple fashion that reflects an urban vibe. When asked in an interview with *Forbes* magazine about his inspiration, Westbrook commented that his favorite part of the design process was, "inspiration. Just pulling inspiration and seeing it come to life is the best part."

Westbrook lives his life under his "Why not?" mantra, believing that no one should tell you what you can or cannot do with your life.

TEXT-DEPENDENT QUESTIONS

1. What is the name of the program that Westbrook, through his foundation, has invested in and that provides literacy opportunities for school-aged children in Oklahoma City?

2. In what city and neighborhood did Westbrook purchase a $19.5 million home? Which NBA star is his neighbor?

3. In which year did he sign a contract extension to remain a member of the Oklahoma City Thunder? How much is the extension worth?

 RESEARCH PROJECT

Westbrook has a passion for reading. He has matched that passion with a desire to help elementary students in Oklahoma City gain even greater access to books. His Why Not? Foundation has built 20 Russell's Reading Rooms at various schools, and he hopes to spread his love of books to even more youth, thus continuing to promote literacy. What other NBA stars are engaged in literacy or other related education projects, either through funding or programs created by their personal foundations? Find three additional examples and explain the name of the program, the star that is providing the support, and the type of students the programs are aimed at (from K–12).

assist: a pass that directly leads to a teammate making a basket.

blocked shot: when a defensive player stops a shot at the basket by hitting the ball away.

center: a player whose main job is to score near the basket and win offensive and defensive rebounds. Centers are usually the tallest players on the court, and the best are able to move with speed and agility.

double-dribble: when a player dribbles the ball with two hands or stops dribbling and starts again. The opposing team gets the ball.

field goal: a successful shot worth two points—three points if shot from behind the three-point line.

foul: called by the officials for breaking a rule: reaching in, blocking, charging, and over the back, for example. If a player commits six fouls during the game, he fouls out and must leave play. If an offensive player is fouled while shooting, he usually gets two foul shots (one shot if the player's basket counted or three if he was fouled beyond the three-point line).

foul shot: a "free throw," an uncontested shot taken from the foul line (15 feet [4.6 m]) from the basket.

goaltending: when a defensive player touches the ball after it has reached its highest point on the way to the basket. The team on offense gets the points they would have received from the basket. Goaltending is also called on any player, on offense or defense, who slaps the backboard or touches the ball directly above the basket.

jump ball: when an official puts the ball into play by tossing it in the air. Two opposing players try to tip it to their own teammate.

man-to-man defense: when each defensive player guards a single offensive player.

officials: those who monitor the action and call fouls. In the NBA there are three for each game.

point guard: the player who handles the ball most on offense. He brings the ball up the court and tries to create scoring opportunities through passing. Good point guards are quick, good passers, and can see the court well.

power forward: a player whose main jobs are to score from close to the basket and win offensive and defensive rebounds. Good power forwards are tall and strong.

rebound: when a player gains possession of the ball after a missed shot.

roster: the players on a team. NBA teams have 12-player rosters.

shooting guard: a player whose main job is to score using jump shots and drives to the basket. Good shooting guards are usually taller than point guards but still quick.

shot clock: a 24-second clock that starts counting down when a team gets the ball. The clock restarts whenever the ball changes possession. If the offense does not shoot the ball in time, it turns the ball over to the other team.

small forward: a player whose main job is to score from inside or outside. Good small forwards are taller than point or shooting guards and have speed and agility.

steal: when a defender takes the ball from an opposing player.

technical foul: called by the official for misconduct or a procedural violation. The team that does not commit the foul gets possession of the ball and a free throw.

three-point play: a two-point field goal combined with a successful free throw. This happens when an offensive player makes a basket but is fouled in the process.

three-point shot: a field goal made from behind the three-point line.

traveling: when a player moves, taking three steps or more, without dribbling, also called "walking." The opposing team gets the ball.

turnover: when the offensive team loses the ball: passing the ball out of bounds, traveling, or double-dribbling, for example.

zone defense: when each defensive player guards within a specific area of the court. Common zones include 2-1-2, 1-3-1, or 2-3. Zone defense has only recently been allowed in the NBA.

FURTHER READING

Doeden, Matt. *Russell Westbrook*. Minneapolis, MN: Lerner Publications, 2017.

Lowe, Jordan. *Russell Westbrook: The Incredible Story of Russell Westbrook—One of Basketball's Greatest Players!* Scotts Valley, CA: Createspace Independent Publishing Platform, 2017.

Mayberry, Darnell, and Perkins, Kendrick. *100 Things Thunder Fans Should Know & Do Before They Die*. Chicago: Triumph Books, 2017.

Nagelhout, Ryan. *Russell Westbrook: Triple-Double Superstar.* New York: Britannica Educational Publishing, 2019.

Westbrook Jr., Russell. *Russell Westbrook: Style Drivers.* New York: Rizzoli International Publications, Incorporated, 2017.

INTERNET RESOURCES

https://www.basketball-reference.com/players/w/westbru01.html
The basketball-specific resource provided by Sports Reference, LLC, for current and historical statistics of Russell Westbrook.

http://bleacherreport.com/nba
The official website for Bleacher Report Sport's NBA reports on each of the 30 teams.

https://www.cbssports.com/nba/teams/OKC/oklahoma-city-thunder/
The web page for the Oklahoma City Thunder provided by CBSSports.com, providing latest news and information, player profiles, scheduling, and standings.

https://newsok.com/sports/thunder
The web page of the Oklahoman (Oklahoma City) newspaper for the Oklahoma City Thunder basketball team.

http://www.espn.com/nba/team/_/name/okc/oklahoma-city-thunder
The official website of ESPN sports network for the Oklahoma City Thunder.

http://www.nba.com/#/
The official website of the National Basketball Association.

http://www.espn.com/nba/team/_/name/okc/oklahoma-city-thunder
The official NBA website for the Oklahoma City Thunder basketball team, including history, player information, statistics, and news.

https://sports.yahoo.com/nba/
The official website of Yahoo! Sports NBA coverage, providing news, statistics, and important information about the association and its 30 teams.

INDEX

INDEX

INDEX

EDUCATIONAL VIDEO LINKS

Pg. 12: http://x-qr.net/1LZb

Pg. 13: http://x-qr.net/1JUH

Pg. 14: http://x-qr.net/1Jk4

Pg. 15: http://x-qr.net/1Kzh

Pg. 16: http://x-qr.net/1Kqm

Pg. 17: http://x-qr.net/1Jah

Pg. 18: http://x-qr.net/1Hzx

Pg. 19: http://x-qr.net/1K3E

Pg. 30: http://x-qr.net/1M5w

Pg. 44: http://x-qr.net/1L0U

Pg. 61: http://x-qr.net/1J3g

Pg. 69: http://x-qr.net/1KhL

PHOTO CREDITS

ABOUT THE AUTHOR

Donald Parker is an avid sports fan, author, and father. He enjoys watching and participating in many types of sports, including football, basketball, baseball, and golf. He enjoyed a brief career as a punter and defensive back at NCAA Division III Carroll College (now University) in Waukesha, Wisconsin, and spends much of his time now watching and writing about the sports he loves.